426
SERIES

THE
INCOMPARABLE
CHRIST

Kit Sublett

Whitecaps Media
Houston, Texas
whitecapsmedia.com

The Incomparable Christ
© 2016 Kit Sublett
All rights reserved

ISBN: 978-1-942732-12-9

Epigraph is from *Young Life* magazine, November 1953

For information on bulk purchases of this book, please visit
whitecapsmedia.com

Printed in the United States of America

Table of Contents

Download the Study Guide
for this book at
whitecapsmedia.com

Jesus Christ is everything that [people]
want most, if they just knew it—
the most wonderful, the most attractive,
the strongest, most gracious, loving person
this world has ever seen.

Jim Rayburn
founder of Young Life

Study 1

He is God

My friend Ted Johnson once told me that "Jesus is the only one we can talk about without fear of exaggeration."

It's true, you know—you can't say enough good things about Jesus. I would go so far as to say that Jesus is incomparable. What does "incomparable" mean? It means that "comparison is impossible," that something or someone is "so outstanding as to be beyond comparison; unsurpassed." Jesus is without compare—He is matchless!

This short four-session Bible study will take a look at four different areas where Christ stands apart. We serve a truly awesome Savior, and it is my hope that these studies will help you to fall more in love with Him than ever before.

The first area we want to look at is a doozie. By itself it sets Jesus apart from everyone else who has ever trod the earth. Put simply it is this: Jesus is God in the flesh (or, as the theologians would say, He is "God incarnate").

Interestingly you can search the four Gospels all day long and you will never find the three words "I am God" coming out of Jesus' mouth. He never said it. At least not using those words.

So if He didn't say the phrase, "I am God," then how can we make that claim about Him? And make no mistake, it is a claim that is central to the Christian faith.

There are several reasons we can make the claim and they form the main part of this study.

1. HE ALMOST SAID IT!

While He didn't say the exact words, "I am God," He came so close that it's really a moot point. While this is clear in a thorough reading of the Gospels, it is especially so in John's, and nowhere more than in John 8.

Jesus gets into quite a quarrel with some Jewish religious leaders. I suggest before you go any further you open your Bible and read the entire exchange. It's only eleven verses—John 8:48–58.

Even before the climax of the story, Jesus is saying things that infuriate his opponents. For instance, "Truly, truly, I say to you, if anyone keeps my word, he will never see death" (8:51).

Now just think about that claim for a second. (Sometimes when we read Scripture we fail to take it at face value and we lose its obvious meaning.) What would you think about a friend who said to you, "If anyone keeps my word, he will never see death"? Who says something like that? Among other things, you would not think your friend was just a good, humble person. At face value, you would almost certainly see your friend the way the Jews saw Jesus: that He (Jesus) was claiming to be more than just a regular person or religious teacher and that He was coming perilously close to claiming deity for Himself.

That they had this opinion is made clear in their response: "Now we know that you have a demon! ... Are you greater than our father Abraham, who died? ... Who do you make yourself out to be?" (8:52–53).

Jesus was certainly not meek and mild that day. He goes right after these guys. "You have not known God," He tells them. Then, to add insult to injury, He says, "I know [God]. If I were to say that I do not know him, I would be a liar like you" (8:55). Yikes! Thems are fightin' words!

Then Jesus says a most interesting thing. The Jews challenge Him by saying, "You are not yet fifty years old, and have you seen Abraham?" (8:57). They were asking this because they knew that Abraham, the father of the Jewish people, had lived generations before and that no one currently alive—especially not a young man like Jesus—could have actually seen Abraham. Jesus' answer draws a dramatic response. After He answers, the Bible tells us that the religious leaders picked up rocks to stone Him to death.

What did He say?

"Jesus said to them, 'Truly, truly, I say to you, before Abraham was, I am' " (8:58).

Now the religious leaders did not want to stone Jesus because they thought He was using bad grammar. They wanted to kill Him because it was clear to them that He had committed blasphemy, that is, that Jesus was claiming to be God.

While that may not be crystal clear to us, it was to the religious leaders of Jesus' day. The phrase "I am" had tremendous biblical significance and both Jesus and the religious leaders knew it. The context is this:

In Exodus 3, God has asked Moses to represent Him to the Israelites. Moses asks God, "If I come to the people of Israel and say to them, 'The God of your fathers has sent me to you,' and they ask me, 'What is his name?' what shall I say to them?' " (Exodus 3:13).

Good question: What is God's name? "God" and "Father" are more titles than they are names. Here is God's response:

> God said to Moses, "I AM WHO I AM." And he said, "Say this to the people of Israel, 'I AM has sent me to you ... This is my name forever, and thus I am to be remembered throughout all generations.'"
>
> *(Exodus 3:14–15)*

So when Jesus said about Himself, "Before Abraham was, I am," the meaning was clear: He was claiming to be God.

One other passage where Jesus comes very close to the words "I am God" (and certainly where that was His meaning) is in John 10.

"I and the Father are one," Jesus declares (John 10:30).

Again, look at that statement at face value. If someone was to say to you that "God and I are one," the implication would be very clear. It certainly was to the Jews. Their response to that statement was the same as they had two chapters earlier: "The Jews picked up stones again to stone him" (John 10:31).

Jesus did indeed claim to be God. Let's continue to look at some reasons we can know not only that He claimed it but that He truly was God in the flesh.

2. HE DID THINGS ONLY GOD CAN DO

If someone comes along and claims to be God (and this has happened numerous times over the years, and not just people who end up in mental institutions!), then it would be natural to expect him or her to do things that only God can do.

Think of all of the things that Jesus did that only God—or someone with God's help—could do. He controlled nature, He raised the dead, He created stuff out of thin air. Every one of the miracles that are recorded in the Gospels speak to Jesus' divinity. Now, the fact that He did miracles does not prove His deity. After all, Jesus empowered the disciples to work miracles in His name and there are instances all through Scripture, in both the Old and New Testaments, of people performing miracles.

The point here is that if someone claimed to be God, then we would expect that person to do things consistent with being God, and that includes things that only God can do.

In addition to the miracles, there is something very significant that Christ did along these lines. The story is told in Matthew 9.

> And getting into a boat he crossed over and came to his own city. And behold, some people brought to him a paralytic, lying on a bed. And when Jesus saw their faith, he said to the paralytic, "Take heart, my son; your sins are forgiven."   *(Matthew 9:1–2)*

Imagine if someone in your Bible study came in and announced, "My friend, your sins are forgiven." What would you think about that person? If you were honest, you would be a little troubled. "Where does she get off saying that she has the power or ability to forgive sins? Who does she think she is?"

To do this would *not* be normal or even acceptable behavior.

The only person who can forgive sins is God. That's because sins are offenses committed against God. Just as you can't forgive me for something bad I did against a third party, so no one can go around forgiving people for offenses they've committed against God Almighty.

Let's continue looking at the story:

> And behold, some of the scribes said to themselves,
> "This man is blaspheming." *(Matthew 9:3)*

Once again we have the same response from the people who were eyewitnesses. It may not be immediately obvious to us that Christ was claiming to do something only God could do, but it was to the people He was with that day.

> But Jesus, knowing their thoughts, said, "Why do you think evil in your hearts? For which is easier, to say, 'Your sins are forgiven,' or to say, 'Rise and walk'?" *(Matthew 9:4–5)*

Don't you just love that Jesus read their minds? A mini-proof of His divinity right there (that's not the only time He did that in Scripture, by the way).

> "But that you may know that the Son of Man has authority on earth to forgive sins"—he then said to the paralytic—'Rise, pick up your bed and go home.' And he rose and went home." *(Matthew 9:6–7)*

It would be easier to say "your sins are forgiven" because there would be no evidence of Jesus' success or failure in that regard. There would be no outward sign that the man had been forgiven. If, on the other hand, Jesus declared the man healed, everyone there could tell right away whether or not Christ could do what He claimed. But the fact that the man was physically healed was visible evidence of Jesus' authority.

3. THE REST OF THE NEW TESTAMENT TESTIFIES TO JESUS' DEITY.
Not only did Jesus say things that indicated He was God and do things that only God could do, but the rest of the New Testament is replete with verses to back that up. Let's take a look at a few of them.

> [Jesus] is the radiance of the glory of God and the exact imprint of his nature, and he upholds the universe by the word of his power. After making purification for sins, he sat down at the right hand of the Majesty on high ...   *(Hebrews 1:3)*

Does that verse sound like it's talking about a mere man? What mere man is the exact imprint of God's nature? Yes, we are made in God's image, but the word used here is different. It's the Greek word *charakter* and it appears in Scripture only in this one place. Here's how

The Living Bible translates it: "all that God's Son is and does marks Him as God" (TLB). Further, what mere man can "uphold the universe by the word of his power"? Jesus was no mere man. He was—and is—God.

There is another passage that we should look at. Look at how the book of Colossians describes Jesus:

> He is the image of the invisible God, the firstborn of all creation. For by him all things were created, in heaven and on earth, visible and invisible, whether thrones or dominions or rulers or authorities—all things were created through him and for him. And he is before all things, and in him all things hold together. *(Colossians 1:15–17)*

There is much to consider in those three verses. One is the purpose of Christ's incarnation—His coming to earth. God is invisible (see John 1:18; Job 9:11; Exodus 33:20). So for us to really understand Him, Christ "became flesh and dwelt among us" (John 1:14). The passage also tells us that Jesus created everything. Who but God could do that? (See also 1 Corinthians 8:6.) But there is something else in that passage—just a single word—that is rather amazing. It says that all things were created *for* Him as well as by Him. Everything on earth was created for His pleasure. That includes us. If we are not living for Christ, then you're not really living. You may think you are, but you're not. True life is found only in Christ.

Paul, the writer of Colossians, continues:

> For in him all the fullness of God was pleased to dwell, and through him to reconcile to himself all things, whether on earth or in heaven, making peace by the blood of his cross.   *(Colossians 1:19–20)*

As if those verses from chapter 1 of Colossians were not enough, Paul doubles down in chapter 2:

> For in [Christ] the whole fullness of deity dwells bodily, and you have been filled in him, who is the head of all rule and authority.   *(Colossians 2:9–10)*

"The whole fullness of deity dwells in him." Wow! Jesus is indeed God in human form.

(For a list of some other verses that attest to the deity of Christ, see the Appendix in the back of this book. There are many more than the ones I have listed, but they're a good start. It would be a good idea to familiarize yourself with these foundational verses.)

4. GOD GAVE JESUS HIS SEAL OF APPROVAL.

You would expect that if someone was going around claiming to be God in the flesh that the Father would have something to say about it, particularly if it was true.

Both God the Father and God the Spirit did indeed say something about it, and nowhere more obviously than in the story of Jesus' baptism.

> And when Jesus was baptized, immediately he went up from the water, and behold, the heavens were opened to him, and he saw the Spirit of God descending like a dove and coming to rest on him; and behold, a voice from heaven said, "This is my beloved Son, with whom I am well pleased."
>
> *(Matthew 3:16–17)*

What a great story! At a crucial launching point of the Son's ministry on earth, the Father and the Spirit announce their approval. While this does not prove Jesus' divinity, it is something you would expect. After all, if God had truly sent His Son to earth, you would think He would signify His approval—and He did. (For a slightly different recounting of the story, see Luke 3:21–22.)

5. HE ACCEPTED PEOPLE'S PRAISE AS GOD

There is one more point that I think proves that the Bible claims that Jesus is God. Two more quick stories in Matthew point this out. The first is one you are probably familiar with. It's the story of Jesus walking on the water (Matthew 14:22–33).

> Immediately he made the disciples get into the boat and go before him to the other side, while he dismissed the crowds. And after he had dismissed the crowds, he went up on the mountains by himself to pray. When evening came, he was there alone, but the boat by this time was a long way from the land, beaten by the waves, for the wind was against them.
>
> *(Matthew 14:22–24)*

While Jesus is having this peaceful time in communion with His Father and the Spirit, the poor disciples are out on the water, no doubt stressed out over the wind and the waves. What Jesus does next is one of the most famous miracles He ever did.

> And in the fourth watch of the night he came to them, walking on the sea. But when the disciples saw him walking on the sea, they were terrified, and said,

"It is a ghost!" and they cried out in fear. But immediately Jesus spoke to them, saying, "Take heart; it is I. Do not be afraid."

And Peter answered him, "Lord, if it is you, command me to come to you on the water." He said, "Come." So Peter got out of the boat and walked on the water and came to Jesus. But when he saw the wind, he was afraid, and beginning to sink he cried out, "Lord, save me." Jesus immediately reached out his hand and took hold of him, saying to him, "O you of little faith, why did you doubt?" And when they got into the boat, the wind ceased.

(Matthew 14:25–32)

Now, "the fourth watch of the night" was probably around 3:00 or 4:00 in the morning, truly the dead of night. This must have been a terrifying experience for the disciples, particularly those who were not used to being out on the water. There was a storm, it was the middle of the night, they were no doubt scared for their lives, and then they see something or Someone walking on the water.

To add to the drama, Peter challenges the water walker to have him come out and join him, which Jesus does. As the disciples strained in the darkness to watch, out goes Peter. First their friend is walking, and then he is sinking!

Jesus saves him and the two of them get on the boat with the others. And that leads up to the key verse for our purposes.

> And those in the boat worshiped him, saying, "Truly you are the Son of God."
>
> And when they had crossed over, they came to land at Gennesaret.   *(Matthew 14:33–34)*

You may wonder why I included verse 34. It's not because of what it tells us, it's because of what it doesn't say. You see, the men in the boat had just *worshiped* Jesus and called him "the Son of God" (not *a* son of God, but *the* Son of God). If someone called me "the Son of God" and worshiped me, there is only one proper response on my part: I would demand that they cut it out. It would not be right for anyone to bow down to me or to any other man as God.

But notice that Jesus does not do this. He accepts their praise. This is incredibly significant. He did not mind people worshiping Him as God—because He is God!

Now let's look at our final short story in Matthew. It takes the point even further.

> Now when Jesus came into the district of Caesarea Philippi, he asked his disciples, "Who do people say that the Son of Man is?" And they said, "Some say John the Baptist, others say Elijah, and others Jeremiah or one of the prophets." He said to them, "But who do you say that I am?" Simon Peter replied, "You are the Christ, the Son of the living God." And Jesus answered him, "Blessed are you, Simon Bar-Jonah! For flesh and blood has not revealed this to you, but my Father who is in heaven."
>
> *(Matthew 16:13–17)*

This time, just a while later, Jesus does say something. And far from being a "Cut it out!" kind of demand, He praised Peter for his observation, telling him that only God the Father could have revealed this to him.

This is not to say that accepting praise as God proves that you are God. There are many people who have done so. But when anyone does, it is either true—he or she really is God—or it is false—he or she is not God. If a person makes this claim and it's not true, then the person either knows he is lying, which means he would be among the worst people who have ever lived, or he does not know he's lying, in which case he would be among the craziest people who have ever lived.

Which is it for Jesus? The great Christian author C. S. Lewis famously spoke about this in his book, *Mere Christianity*:

> I am trying here to prevent anyone saying the really foolish thing that people often say about him: I'm ready to accept Jesus as a great moral teacher, but I don't accept his claim to be God. That is the one thing we must not say. A man who was merely a man and said the sort of things Jesus said would not be a great moral teacher. He would either be a lunatic—on the level with the man who says he is a poached egg—or else he would be the Devil of Hell. You must make your choice. Either this man was, and is, the Son of God, or else a madman or something worse. You can shut him up for a fool, you can spit at him and kill him as a demon or you can fall at his feet and call him Lord and God, but let us not come with any patronizing nonsense about his being a great human teacher. He has not left that open to us. He did not intend to.

As Jesus asked His disciples so now He asks you, "Who do *you* say that I am?"

His Nativity and Incarnation

The purpose of this series is to look at a few of the things that make Jesus unique and without compare, some of the reasons we can call Him "the incomparable Christ." Our first study looked at the fact that Jesus is God in human form. In this next chapter we are going to talk about two related topics: His nativity and His incarnation.

You might be thinking, "I don't even know what those words mean!" But, without even consulting a dictionary or the internet, you can probably figure out their meanings.

If you speak Spanish, you're halfway to understanding what "incarnation" means. *Carne* is Spanish for meat or flesh. You probably know that the prefix "in-" means into, within, or just good old in. When you add

"-ion" to something it means an action or process. So putting "in-" together with "carne" and "-ion" you get a word that means "the act of putting on flesh," or, more specific to the Christian faith, "the doctrine that God the Son became man." (You can also see the meaning in the word "reincarnation," which means to put a new body on.)

Our other word, "nativity," might be easier to understand if you think of its related word, "native." To be a native of somewhere (in my case, Texas) means that you were born there. Nativity simply means birth. You have a nativity story, I have a nativity story … we all have nativity stories. Maybe your parents had to rush to the hospital, or you were born in the backseat of a cab. It may or may not be dramatic, but you do have a nativity story. The Nativity (capitalized and with "the" in front of it) refers to the most incredible birth story of all time—the birth of Jesus. The Nativity is the vehicle by which the Incarnation happened. So the words are closely related and we're going to take a look at them in this study. They are part of what makes Christ someone without compare or equal.

Let's talk about the Nativity first.

If a store is normally open twenty-four hours a day, what is the one day of the year it might be closed?

Christmas day. The entire world seems to stop at Christmastime! That's because we're celebrating the most important birthday of all time, the birthday of Jesus.

Now, even if you think that Jesus is important, it may seem odd that His birthday would be cause for so much celebration. But when you consider that His birth meant the coming of God to our planet, and was therefore a truly unique event, then it becomes clearer why the celebration of the Nativity is such a big deal.

You might expect such a momentous event would have been predicted in the Old Testament, and you would be correct. There are many prophecies concerning the life of Jesus that were made hundreds of years before His appearance, and several of them have to do specifically with the Nativity. We'll look at three of them in this study.

> "Therefore the Lord himself will give you a sign. Behold the virgin shall conceive and bear a son, and shall call his name Immanuel." *(Isaiah 7:14)*

If you are familiar with the Christmas story, then Isaiah 7:14 will have a familiar ring to it. It is cited in Matthew 1:23 where Matthew points out for us that in Hebrew the word *Immanuel* means "God with us."

That's rather significant to this whole notion of incarnation, isn't it? Jesus is "God with us." Wow! (You might wonder, though, "Why does it say His name will be Immanuel when we know they called Him Jesus?" The idea is that Immanuel is one of the many titles that Jesus holds, along with Son of Man, the Truth, the Son of God, and others, including the list of names He is given in the next verse we will look at. Immanuel may not have appeared on His birth certificate—if they had had those back in His day, which they did not—but if you call Him Immanuel when you see Him in heaven, He will respond!)

We know from the New Testament that Mary was a virgin when she gave birth to Jesus. A unique event, to be sure, and just as Isaiah had promised!

A very famous Old Testament prediction of Jesus' birth comes from Isaiah 9:

> For to us a child is born,
>> to us a son is given;
> and the government shall be upon his shoulder,
>> and his name shall be called
> Wonderful Counselor, Mighty God,
>> Everlasting Father, Prince of Peace.
>
> *(Isaiah 9:6)*

You might recognize this passage not from the Bible but from a chorus in Handel's "Messiah." The song is often performed at Christmas. If you aren't familiar with it and can stand classical music, look up "Handel For Unto Us" on the internet and you will be blessed. It's one of the greatest pieces of music ever written.

As you get to know Christ better, you will see how perfectly He fulfills those titles: Wonderful Counselor, Mighty God, Everlasting Father, and Prince of Peace.

One last passage that clearly predicts the events of Jesus' birth is in Micah:

> But you, O Bethlehem Ephrathah,
>> who are too little to be among the clans of
>> Judah,
> from you shall come forth for me
>> one who is to be ruler in Israel,
> whose coming forth is from of old,
>> from ancient days.

(Micah 5:2)

The thing that almost certainly stands out in your mind as you read this passage looking for similarities to what we know of Christmas is Bethlehem, and you would be correct.

Some background will be helpful to understand the significance of this prediction a little better. Bethlehem was, and still is, a small town, less than ten miles away from the much more significant and important city of Jerusalem. Think of a small town near your own and you might have a good idea of the oddity that the future ruler of all Israel (and indeed the world) was prophesied to be born in Bethlehem rather than Jerusalem. Jerusalem was the capital city. Jerusalem was where the Temple was. It would be like if the future King of England were to be born in Honiton rather than in London. (Haven't heard of Honiton? I hadn't either until I visited friends there ... and that's my point. As Honiton in England is not prominent, neither was Bethlehem in Judea.)

But Bethlehem was not a random choice by God for His Son's entry point on earth. First, though small, Bethlehem did have historical significance. It was nicknamed the City of David because Israel's great king, David, had been anointed there. It was appropriate, then, that Jesus would be born in Bethlehem as the Messiah was to be a descendant of David (see John 7:42). In addition to that, the name Bethlehem offers a clue as to its choice for Jesus' birth story. In Hebrew *bethlehem* means "House of Bread." Why might that be important? I believe that God orchestrated the naming of the town. I believe He named it not after King David, an obvious choice, but after a greater King—One who was to follow David—who would be the King of Kings; the One who said of Himself, "I am the bread of life; whoever comes to me shall not hunger, and whoever believes in me shall never thirst" (John 6:35). Bethlehem is the "House of the Bread of Life, Jesus."

List out all of the details you know from the story of Jesus' arrival here on earth. Even someone with a cursory knowledge of the Bible is most likely aware of some of them: Mary, Joseph, the stable, the manger, the shepherds, the "Three Kings of the Orient" (a.k.a. "The Three Wise Men"), gold, frankincense, and myrrh. The list goes on. And all of them are weighted with symbolism.

It makes sense, doesn't it? If God was indeed going to come to earth, He would no doubt make it special and would have taken great care, thought, and planning in its execution.

The reasons for some of the details are fairly easy to understand. The fact that He was greeted by both kings and lowly shepherds, for instance, indicated that He was to be King of all. The fact that He was born in a stable signaled to us that He was a humble servant.

But some of the meaning isn't obvious at first glance. Take a moment to put yourself in Mary and Joseph's shoes. What must it have been like to have been young, unmarried, expecting a child, and turned away from any suitable lodging? What shame did they carry with them? Did Joseph believe Mary's story of being a virgin? How did Mary feel, knowing that her child was to be the Savior of the world (as she had been told in Luke 1:31–35)?

And other elements of the Nativity carry symbolism not obvious to the casual observer. For instance, in my mind it is no accident that Jesus was welcomed by shepherds. Experts point out that it is likely the sheep those shepherds were watching over weren't just any sheep—they were lambs slated to be used for sacrifices. Can you see the symbolism there? (See John 1:29.)

And there is still yet more symbolism at play with those shepherds. You see, according to scholars, shepherds in those days carried a reputation for being thieves. So at His birth, surrounded by shepherds/thieves, you see a foreshadowing of His death—where He would be the ultimate sacrificial Lamb, surrounded once again by thieves.

Say what you will, this much is sure: No one ever came into this world the same way that Jesus did!

The final thing to observe about His nativity is the idea of the Virgin Birth. As we read earlier in Isaiah 7:14, it was predicted that the Savior would be born of a virgin.

Both Matthew (see 1:23) and Luke (see 1:26–27) tell us that Mary was a virgin when she gave birth to Jesus. This is important for a few reasons, not the least of which is that it is one more prophecy that Jesus fulfilled (fulfilling Isaiah 7:14).

Another reason the virgin birth is important is that it points to the two sides of Jesus' nature. He was fully God and fully Man. He had to be, in order to fulfill His unique role in history, which leads us to our next topic to consider: His incarnation.

Take a look at John 1:14:

> And the Word became flesh and dwelt among us, and we have seen his glory, glory as of the only Son from the Father, full of grace and truth.

The Word—that's Jesus—became flesh, that is, He put on a human body. Not just that, but He left the comforts of heaven and came here and "dwelt among us." The literal translation of that phrase in the original Greek means He "pitched a tent among us."

Can you think of all the ways that this is significant? A few come to my mind. Here's one: There are religions and belief systems that say God is distant and uncaring. The Incarnation stands directly opposed to that. God didn't just set the world to spinning and walk away. He came here Himself! He walked among us. He lived a full life here and entered into our mess in a very real, historic way.

Which brings up another reason the Incarnation is important: It is a historic event. The God we worship is not an idea or a concept. He is real. He came here. We can see where He lived, the streets He walked, and the places where He did His miracles.

Here's another thing. By coming here, God gives this world His seal of approval. He is not fooled, of course— He knows it's not perfect—but by choosing to put on skin and be one of us, He is saying that mankind—all of mankind—has value.

Fourthly, Jesus can identify with us. He knows what it's like to laugh, to cry, to be hungry, to be tired. He also knows what it's like to have friends, to have heartache, to lose a parent (there are good reasons to believe that Joseph died when Jesus was young), and to be deserted by His friends. He was born in an oppressed country so He knows what it's like to be in a minority.

He counted poor people, religious people, wealthy people, and laborers as His acquaintances and friends. This is all because He experienced life fully, in person.

One of the best verses about Christ's incarnation is this one:

> [Jesus], though he was in the form of God, did not count equality with God a thing to be grasped [in the sense of holding on to], but made himself nothing, taking the form of a servant, being born in the likeness of men. And being found in human form, he humbled himself by becoming obedient to the point of death, even death on a cross. *(Philippians 2:6–8)*

In addition to subjecting Himself to being born, to having to learn to walk and to talk, to being hungry and thirsty, ultimately Jesus even submitted Himself to an unfair trial and prosecution and suffered death.

Jesus played by the same rules He gave us!

You'll notice that the verse says He did not consider equality with God as something to be grasped or held on to. Isn't that amazing? I am not an expert on other religions, but this idea of God taking on human skin and walking among us seems pretty unusual. What an amazing God we serve!

A side note: The next time you think you're something special and that you're better than someone else, just remember how our Example lived His life. We too should be willing to humble ourselves and serve others.

So what was the purpose for all of this? We can see that in 1 Timothy:

> For there is one God, and there is one mediator between God and men, the man Christ Jesus, who gave himself as a ransom for all, which is the testimony given at the proper time. *(1 Timothy 2:5–6)*

I have a friend who practices a branch of the law called mediation (notice, that's mediation, not meditation—she doesn't get paid to sit and contemplate all day!). People who are at odds with one another come to her, hash out their differences, and she helps them come to an agreed-upon resolution. She is a mediator.

The dictionary defines mediator as "one that reconciles differences between disputants" ("disputants" meaning people engaged in a dispute). First Timothy tells us that the greatest mediator is Jesus Himself.

As far as the Bible is concerned, the ultimate broken relationship is between Man and God. The problem is

Man's sin. You'll notice that, unlike most of the parties my friend serves as a mediator for, only one party is guilty when it comes to the relationship between mankind and God: us. God has never been in the wrong and never will be. All of the wrongdoing is on our side.

This is where the Incarnation is so important. Christ was both God and Man. And as such He was able to stand between the two sides and settle our differences.

Two verses use the word "enemies" to describe our relationship toward God, and both of them come to the same conclusion: It is only because of Christ's mediation that we are able to have peace with God.

> For if while we were enemies we were reconciled to God by the death of his Son, much more, now that we are reconciled, shall we be saved by his life.
>
> *(Romans 5:10)*

> [You] were once far away from God. You were his enemies, separated from him by your evil thoughts and actions. Yet now he has reconciled you to himself through the death of Christ in his physical body. As a result, he has brought you into his own presence, and you are holy and blameless as you stand before him without a single fault.
>
> *(Colossians 1:21–22, NLT)*

The story of our reconciliation with God is further explained in 2 Corinthians 5:17–21. The first part of that passage is one of my favorites.

> Therefore, if anyone is in Christ, he is a new creation. The old has passed away, behold the new has come.
>
> *(2 Corinthians 5:17)*

That's a verse I hope you're familiar with (or you should be, at least). If you have not begun memorizing Scripture, you should—there are few things you can do that will help you more—and this is a great verse to begin with. The next verses give us added context, picking up the theme of reconciliation.

> All this is from God, who through Christ reconciled us to himself and gave us the ministry of reconciliation. That is, in Christ God was reconciling the world to himself, not counting their trespasses against them, and entrusting to us the message of reconciliation. Therefore, we are ambassadors for Christ, God making his appeal through us. We implore you on behalf of Christ, be reconciled to God. For our sake he made him to be sin who knew no sin, so that in him we might become the righteousness of God.
>
> *(2 Corinthians 5:18–21)*

As a man, Jesus was a perfect representative for us. As the Son of God and one of the members of the Trinity, He was able to represent the other side of the equation. And as the Son of God, His death was acceptable as payment on behalf of all of us.

Lastly, take a look at Mark 10:45:

> [Jesus said,] "For even the Son of Man came not to be served but to serve, and to give his life as a ransom for many."

What do you think motivated Jesus to die for us? John 3:16 tells us His motivation was that He loved us.

Jesus' incarnation—His putting on flesh and living among us—and His nativity allowed Him to be both our mediator and our ransom.

A few quick notes concerning questions that may arise on this topic. The first is that someone might point out that scholars do not believe Jesus was born on December 25. Actually, that presents no problem to the Bible at all, as Scripture does not give a date for Jesus' birth. When we as Christians celebrate Christmas day, we are celebrating the *event* of His nativity, not its date. We do this all the time with belated (or early) birthday parties. In fact, in England Queen Elizabeth's birthday has been celebrated for decades in June, even though her actual birth date is in April (this is done in order to ensure better weather for the attendant parade).

Another note: Though Joseph functioned as Jesus' earthly father, he was not in fact Jesus' father. God was. Matthew 1:20 recounts that Joseph was told by an angel, "Joseph, son of David, do not fear to take Mary as your wife, for that which is conceived in her is from the Holy Spirit." Luke 1:35 also addresses this.

Finally, many speculate that Joseph died when Jesus was young. That is because we see no mention of him in the Gospels after Jesus' visit to the temple when the Savior was twelve years old, while we do have further mentions of Mary. Almost certainly Joseph died between the time Jesus was twelve and the time He began His public ministry around the age of thirty (Luke 3:23).

Study 3

His Treatment of Others

You can tell a lot about people by the way they treat others. I had a friend once—an acquaintance, really—who claimed to be a Christian. Early on in my relationship with this guy, I began to notice the way he treated "the little people"—secretaries and waiters, for instance. He was downright rude. Meanwhile, I noticed that when he was around someone who was a big shot, he kowtowed to them.

I knew then and there to be wary of him. My assessment proved to be correct, as he ended up hurting a lot of people who worked with him, all the while loudly proclaiming his Christianity.

On the other hand, I also remember the positive example of my friend Pat. When he reached retirement age, his wife put on a nice party for him. It was inspiring to see all types of people, from former bosses, employees, neighbors, and even his own children, rise to give testimony to what a wonderful example he had been to them. Pat was someone who took his faith seriously and it showed in his life and in his treatment of others.

We have been looking at how Jesus is without compare, and here's one more area where He's incomparable: the way He treated people when He was here on earth.

Jesus famously interacted with all types of people. Fishermen, religious leaders, prostitutes, lepers, His family, regular people, military men, children, and government officials, to name a few.

If you think about all of those stories in the Gospels of His interactions with people of all types, you will see that, while He was harsh with some people, He was kind and gracious to many more. But He treated all of them fairly. He was only harsh with those whose behavior merited it.

That's because "God shows no partiality" (Romans 2:11). So if Jesus was God in human form, it is to be expected that He would show no partiality or favoritism.

In this study we're going to look at three stories of Jesus interacting with different types of people. The first is the account of Jesus and a man named Zacchaeus. It's found in the first ten verses of Luke 19.

> He entered Jericho and was passing through. And behold, there was a man named Zacchaeus. He was a chief tax collector and was rich.   *(Luke 19:1–2)*

Jericho was a major intersection back then, and as such it was a major toll collection point. Zacchaeus, or Zach for short, was the "chief tax collector" and had gotten very wealthy from his work for the Roman government.

To understand the significance of Zach's job, it's helpful to know that tax collectors, more than just about any other profession, were singled out in Jesus' day as bad guys. Before we go further with Zach's story, take a look at this account from Matthew to get an idea of how they were viewed:

> As Jesus passed on from there, he saw a man called Matthew sitting at the tax booth, and he said to him, "Follow me." And he rose and followed him.
>
> And as Jesus reclined at table in the house, behold, many tax collectors and sinners came and were reclining with Jesus and his disciples. And

when the Pharisees saw this, they said to his disciples, "Why does your teacher eat with tax collectors
and sinners?" *(Matthew 9:9–11)*

Do you see their disgust with Matthew and his
friends? They can't stand that Jesus is eating not just
with mere "sinners," but specifically "tax collectors."
(By the way, feel free to read verses 12 through 14 for
Jesus' response to the religious leaders' disgust.) There
were reasons for the Pharisees' hatred of tax collectors.
I can think of at least three: First, they collected taxes.
Even today that's not a popular occupation! Second,
they worked with the Roman government (who had
conquered Israel), which is to say they were viewed as
traitors to their own country. And lastly, they often
extorted people—that is, charged them more than
what was owed—and kept the extra money.

With that context, let's go back to the story in Luke.

And he [Zach] was seeking to see who Jesus was, but
on account of the crowd he could not, because he
was small in stature. So he ran on ahead and climbed
up into a sycamore tree to see him, for he was about
to pass that way. *(Luke 19:3–4)*

Zacchaeus was a grown man (albeit a short one). Speaking as a grown man myself, I can tell you that most of us do not climb trees, at least not in public. But Zach must have really wanted to see Jesus. And he was rewarded for his trouble. Look at the next verse:

> And when Jesus came to the place, he looked up and said to him, "Zacchaeus, hurry and come down, for I must stay at your house today." *(Luke 19:5)*

Can you imagine how that made Zach feel? Perhaps there was an initial twinge of embarrassment when the crowd, thanks to Jesus, noticed that he was up in a tree, but more than anything, I think it made Zacchaeus feel great. Look at those words: "I must stay at your house today."

Notice, too, what those words tell us about Jesus. He knew Zach's name! How in the world did He do that? I can think of three ways: He did some research ahead of time about people he might encounter in Jericho; He asked someone when He saw the man in the tree; or most likely, He knew Zach's name already because He's God! But whether He knew it or found it out, the important thing is that He knew it! To Jesus, Zacchaeus was someone worth knowing.

The world's stereotype of God is that He would prefer to spend His time with Goody Two-Shoes types and self-righteous people. However that's not the image we get in the Bible itself, particularly when Jesus is around. Zacchaeus has done nothing righteous or religious to attract Jesus' attention. The only thing I can see that he has done is to show an interest in Him. Not only that, but the cultural context tells us that Zach was far from a religious, holy person.

That tells me a wonderful thing about Jesus: He accepts us where we are. He doesn't necessarily want us to stay there—"Zacchaeus, hurry and come down"— but He accepts us the way we are. He invites us to come follow Him "while we were yet sinners" (Romans 5:8).

One of the great Christians of the 1800s was a preacher named D. L. Moody. He had a very easy-to-understand way of speaking. Here's what he had to say about Zacchaeus:

> There are some people in this nineteenth century who do not believe in sudden conversions. I should like them to tell me where Zacchaeus was converted. He certainly was not converted when he went up into the tree; he certainly *was* converted when he came down. He must have been converted somewhere

between the branches and the ground. The Lord converted him just right there.

Zach's story continues:

So [Zacchaeus] hurried and came down and received [Jesus] joyfully. And when they saw it, they all grumbled, "He has gone in to be the guest of a man who is a sinner." *(Luke 19:6–7)*

Just as Jesus' treatment of Zach tells us a lot about Him, so the others mentioned in the story (the ones who "all grumbled") reveal a lot about themselves by their reaction. That didn't deter Zacchaeus' joy, however. Here's how he responded to Jesus' treatment of him:

And Zacchaeus stood and said to the Lord, "Behold, Lord, the half of my goods I give to the poor. And if I have defrauded anyone of anything, I restore it fourfold." *(Luke 19:8)*

Zach's enthusiasm for Jesus' acceptance of him tells me two things: First, he understood his own sin and his need to allow the Lord to change his life. Second, it makes me wonder if I need to do that myself. Think what a powerful testimony it was for Zach to return *fourfold* any funds that he had extorted! People knew he was sincere because he put his money where his mouth was, so to speak. Are people seeing the same sincerity in me as I claim to follow Jesus?

> And Jesus said to him, "Today salvation has come to this house, since he also is a son of Abraham. For the Son of Man came to seek and to save the lost."
>
> *(Luke 19:9–10)*

Jesus is so awesome! He left heaven and visited earth not just to save the lost, but to *seek* and to save them. He searches us out. He accepts us where and how we are. But He also sees in us something more than we see ourselves, and that leads us to our second story.

This is a short story and it is how Jesus called the first of His twelve disciples. We'll look at the story as it is recounted in Matthew, but Luke 5:1–11 gives more detail if you want to check it out. Here it is in Matthew's account:

> While walking by the Sea of Galilee, he saw two brothers, Simon (who is called Peter) and Andrew

> his brother, casting a net into the sea, for they were
> fishermen. *(Matthew 4:18)*

So you see right away the first people involved in this story: Simon (better known by the nickname that Jesus would give him, "Peter") and his brother Andrew. They were fishermen. Then, as now, fishing was a respectable and necessary occupation, but hardly a prestigious one.

> And he said to them, "Follow me, and I will make you
> fishers of men." Immediately they left their nets and
> followed him. And going on from there he saw two
> other brothers, James the son of Zebedee and John
> his brother, in the boat with Zebedee their father,
> mending their nets, and he called them. Immediately
> they left the boat and their father and followed him.
> *(Matthew 4:19–22)*

In very short order, Peter and Andrew are joined by another pair of brothers, James and John. (Meanwhile, poor old Zebedee, their father, was left to mend the nets on his own!) Those four became the first apostles. Some church denominations call them St. Peter, St. Andrew, St. James, and St. John, and over the centuries everything from cities to hospitals to colleges and churches have been named in their honor. I'm thinking, for instance, of St. Peter's Basilica in Rome (the world's largest church), the city of Santiago, Chile (named after the Spanish version of James's name), the island of Saint John in the Virgin Islands—even the famous golf course at St. Andrew's in Scotland. Not bad for four fishermen!

These four were not honored because they fished for fish. The world may have only seen them as fishermen, but Christ saw in them something even greater. He said they would become "fishers of men." And so they did. As they followed Christ, both before and after His crucifixion and resurrection, the Lord used them to lead countless people to Himself. It is no exaggeration to say that they, along with the other early disciples, turned the world upside down!

When Christ sees you, He doesn't just see what you are. He sees what you can become in Him. He wants us to be the best we can be (which is only possible in relationship with Him). He usually doesn't do this all at once. It takes time (study the story of the twelve apostles in the New Testament and that becomes obvious). Allow Him to challenge you, to mold your life, to change you. You won't regret it.

And along the way you will most certainly make mistakes. How Jesus deals with that is the theme of our final story, the story of Jesus and Peter. We have already seen the moment where Peter began to follow Christ. He quickly became Jesus' chief lieutenant, the leader of the Twelve (for more on that, see Matthew 16:16–19). Peter was a bold follower of Jesus and a great leader for Him, but there was an episode in his life where far from being a leader for Christ, he denied even knowing Him.

After three years of public ministry (during most of which Peter was at His side), Jesus knew His time on earth was coming to an end. The disciples, of course, did not understand exactly what was going to happen, even though Jesus had warned them about it a few times. The night Jesus was betrayed and was heading for His death, He told the disciples some of what lay ahead. Tensions were high, and the situation was confusing. Jesus told Peter He had prayed that Peter's faith would not fail him. That led to this exchange:

> Peter said to [Jesus], "Lord, I am ready to go with you both to prison and to death." Jesus said, "I tell you, Peter, the rooster will not crow this day, until you deny three times that you know me." *(Luke 22:33–34)*

That must have made Peter feel horrible. But what would happen next would make him feel even worse, because it proved just how well Jesus understood His friend Peter.

> Then they seized [Jesus] and led him away, bring-ing him into the high priest's house, and Peter was following at a distance. And when they had kindled a fire in the middle of the courtyard and sat down together, Peter sat down among them. Then a ser-vant girl, seeing him as he sat in the light and look-ing closely at him, said, "This man also was with him." But he denied it, saying, "Woman, I do not know him." *(Luke 22:54–57)*

Peter's accuser was a young woman, a servant girl. She was not anyone that he should have been scared of, and yet he immediately denied Jesus when she ques-tioned him. You can almost hear the defensiveness in his voice as he responds to her, "Woman, I do not know him." But it gets worse.

> And a little later someone else saw him and said, "You also are one of them." But Peter said, "Man, I am not." *(Luke 22:58)*

Strike 2! Peter was not finished yet, of course. The next few verses are heartbreaking to read, even all these years later.

> And after an interval of about an hour still another insisted, saying, "Certainly this man also was with him, for he too is a Galilean." But Peter said, "Man, I do not know what you are talking about." And immediately, while he was still speaking, the rooster crowed. And the Lord turned and looked at Peter. And Peter remembered the saying of the Lord, how he had said to him, "Before the rooster crows today, you will deny me three times." And he went out and wept bitterly. *(Luke 22:59–62)*

Strike 3, just as Jesus had predicted. But don't be too quick to pick on Peter. I think he represents a lot of us who have fallen prey to peer pressure and denied Christ in any number of ways. Can you honestly say that you have never turned your back on Jesus? I wish I could, but I know I have not always been bold and loyal.

Fortunately, it's not the end of the story, for Peter or for us. The last chapter of John's Gospel tells us the beautiful story of Christ's restoration of Peter.

By this time Jesus has risen from the dead. In this particular resurrection appearance, the disciples are by the Sea of Galilee and Jesus has prepared a meal for them.

> When they had finished breakfast, Jesus said to Simon Peter, "Simon, son of John, do you love me more than these?" He said to him, "Yes; Lord, you know that I love you." He said to him, "Feed my lambs." *(John 21:15)*

This was not the first time Peter and the boys had seen Jesus since His miraculous resurrection. Peter had no doubt apologized to his Lord for his denial, and now Jesus singles him out and asks him if he loves Him. He wasn't through.

> He said to him a second time, "Simon, son of John, do you love me?" He said to him, "Yes, Lord; you know that I love you." He said to him, "Tend my sheep." He said to him the third time, "Simon, son of John, do you love me?" Peter was grieved because he said to him the third time, "Do you love me?" and he said to

him, "Lord, you know everything; you know that I love you." Jesus said to him, "Feed my sheep."

(John 21:16–17)

What are we to make of this exchange? While it obviously hurt Peter's feelings, on closer inspection I am sure he eventually saw the beautiful reason for His Savior's repetition. Peter's public proclamation of his love for Jesus reversed his public denial of Him. Peter, already forgiven by the cross, was restored in his own mind and that of the disciples into good fellowship with Christ. Peter indeed did love Jesus, and stayed loyal to Him for the rest of his life, even actually dying rather than deny Him again.

Jesus is incomparable. No one treats people like He did, and still does! For our part, we should try to do the same. We should be known as people who accept others where they are, who believe in what others can be in Christ, and also forgive them when they mess up.

The way Jesus treated others can be summed up in His own "golden rule." He told His followers—and that now includes us—"As you wish that others would do to you, do so to them" (Luke 6:31). If it's good enough for Jesus, it's certainly good enough for us!

Jesus is the Life

What is it with Christians and the word "life"? Off the top of my head I can think of ministries with names like Young Life, Campus Life, Here's Life, New Life, Men's Life, and Abundant Life. You can no doubt add some of your own to that list. It seems we Christians can't get enough of that life deal.

We have been talking about "the incomparable Christ." Our Savior truly is without compare! No one treated people better than He did. No one ever came to the earth the way He did or lived a life like His. And He is uniquely both God and Man. This final study on the incomparable Christ will serve as a summation: *Christ is the life!*

My good old American Heritage Dictionary gives several definitions of "life." Three of them can be summed up with words that begin with the letter E: Existence, Experience, and Eternity.

The reason Christians are so big on life is because that's what Jesus is all about—life in every way, but particularly these three.

Existence is just the idea of life itself. My dictionary describes that aspect of life as "the property or quality that distinguishes living organisms from dead organisms." You know, LIFE, as in existing and being alive, as opposed to being inanimate, dead, or non-existent.

By *experience*, I mean the quality of life, or, as my dictionary puts it, "the physical, mental, and spiritual experiences that constitute existence." So, more than just existing, we're now adding a qualitative aspect to it.

And *eternity* takes our earthly lives into a whole other dimension. The fancy dictionary definition would be "a spiritual state regarded as a transcending of corporeal death." You might have to get a dictionary yourself just to understand that definition, but you really don't need to; eternal life means a life with God that never ends.

When Jesus says He is the life, He means all three aspects: existence, experience, and eternity. This idea is throughout the New Testament, but nowhere is it more emphasized than in the Gospel of John so that's where we'll spend most of our time in this study.

Let's take a look at each of those aspects of life and how Jesus truly is life, starting with John 1:1–4:

In the beginning was the Word, and the Word was with God, and the Word was God. He was in the beginning with God. All things were made through him, and without him was not any thing made that was made. In him was life, and the life was the light of men.

"The Word" in that verse means Jesus (see verse 14). You will notice therefore, that the verse declares that Jesus is God, that He was with the Father and the Spirit from the beginning, and that He made everything. It caps off with the declaration that "in him was life."

Taken together, it is clear that John 1 tells us that Jesus is the source of *all* of life.

Whether a person's first experience with death is that of a beloved pet or a relative, the first time you are faced with death you realize just how fragile life is, and the permanence of death. No amount of medicine or therapy or begging can bring something that is dead back to life. We can take life, we can heal and prolong life, but we cannot animate it. Only God can do that.

Why? Because only God (and that includes Jesus) is the source of life. Only He has life to give. (Lest you think that having a child is giving someone life, the fact is that we cannot do that by our will. Think of all the couples who have trouble conceiving a child. It's not something that we can entirely control; only God can do that.)

In John 5, Jesus addressed this:

> [Jesus said,] "For as the Father raises the dead and gives them life, so also the Son gives life to whom he will." *(John 5:21)*

> [Jesus said,] "For as the Father has life in himself, so he has granted the Son also to have life in himself."
> *(John 5:26)*

That's a ridiculous claim to make about yourself, as Jesus does in those verses. *Unless it's true.* If someone's saying stuff like that you would expect them to be able to prove it, and Jesus did. In fact, He proved it multiple times.

In Luke 7:11–15 we have the account of Jesus raising the son of a widow. One chapter later, in Luke 8, we have the story of Jesus raising the daughter of Jairus. There is also the dramatic story in John 11 of our Lord raising Lazarus from the grave. Finally, each of the Gospels tell the cornerstone miracle of Scripture: the resurrection from the dead of Jesus Himself.

Quite simply, Jesus proved that He is the source of life by reanimating dead people. Wow! (Additionally, both Peter and Paul each raised someone from the dead. It is important to note, though, that they did not claim the ability to do so on their own, as Jesus had done. Given all we know of Peter and Paul, we can be sure they credited Jesus Himself for these resurrections. Two of the three resurrection experiences in the Old Testament came as a direct result of asking God to raise the dead person to life, in other words, the prophets involved did not have or claim the power of life. The third account—in 2 Kings 13—does not directly attribute the power to Elisha himself and there is no need to do so.)

Jesus is not just the source of all life (existence), He is also the source of the best life (that is, experience).

A beloved verse is John 10:10:

> [Jesus said,] "The thief comes only to steal and kill and destroy. I came that they may have life and have it abundantly."

The idea of "abundant life" in the original Greek is that of life with superabundance, in other words, with Christ we do not merely exist and have what we need to survive, but we *abound*—we have life to its fullest possible experience.

Along these lines, Jesus said,

"I am the way, and the truth, and the life."

(John 14:6a)

Think about that! Christ said, plainly, "I am the life." Not, "I know about life," or "I know the way to life," but "I am life itself."

There are serious implications to that. First, it means that apart from Jesus, there is no life (see John 15:5). It also means that if you're not plugged in with Jesus, to quote Young Life's founder Jim Rayburn, you're not living, you're just moving! If you are plugged in with Jesus, then and only then can you begin to know what life is all about.

I have heard many people testify to the idea that their lives only truly began when they met Jesus. Maybe you have heard some of those stories yourself, or maybe that has also been your own experience. For me, I can state without any doubt that my life is *always* better when I am walking with Jesus. It may not be easier or more pleasant, but it is better. There is a difference!

Looking back at all of the men and women of the New Testament, you can't find anyone who regretted following Jesus. In fact, history and tradition teach us that after the resurrection the eleven remaining disciples faced great persecution and most went to their deaths for their beliefs, but none of them denied Christ. The apostle Paul wrote, "For to me to live is Christ, and to die is gain" (Philippians 1:21). There is no reason any of us could ever have to regret following Jesus (see Mark 10:29–30). Quite the opposite: regret comes from those times when we choose *not* to follow Christ. Christ is "the Author of life" (Acts 3:15). As such, He is the one who knows best how to live it!

And that takes us to the third and final area we want to look at in this study: Jesus is the source of eternal life.

Have you ever thought about what "eternal life" means? If you're like me, you might have thought it meant something like "to live forever in heaven." It turns out that, though that is a part of it, it's not the entire proper definition. For that, we can look at what Jesus (who else?) said. In the seventeenth chapter of John Jesus prays what has become known as the "High Priestly Prayer." Jesus' prayer to His Father fills the entire chapter, but He gives a definition of eternal life right at the beginning.

> "And this is eternal life, that they know you the only true God, and Jesus Christ whom you have sent."
>
> *(John 17:3)*

Isn't it interesting that in His definition He does not mentions death, nor does He mention a length of time? Instead, He defines eternal life in a relational way. Eternal life is all tied up in knowing God, through Christ. The idea of "knowing" here is not merely intellectual understanding, but more of a relationship experience.

And when does that begin? Again, Jesus is our source for the correct answer. Look at what He said in John 5:24:

> "Truly, truly, I say to you, whoever hears my word and believes in him who sent me has eternal life. He does not come into judgment, but has passed from death to life."

It is clear in both this verse and also in John 17:3 that eternal life does not begin upon death, but it begins in the here and now, when we are still very much alive on earth. Notice the expression, "has eternal life." That's a present-tense thing, not just a promise of something to come in the future (that would be "shall have eternal life"). To hammer that point home, Jesus says that, upon belief, we have "passed from death to life." Again, describing our present reality. If you believe in Jesus, you have already begun living eternally!

It is no mystery to us as to how biological life begins, but I think most people are misinformed as to how eternal life begins. Again, we'll look at what Jesus said about it:

> [Jesus said,] "I am the living bread that came down from heaven. If anyone eats of this bread, he will live forever. And the bread that I will give for the life of the world is my flesh." *(John 6:51)*

I am sure that Jesus' words were confusing to the first people who heard Him make this declaration. We, however, have the advantage of living after the rest of the events of His life. Therefore, we know that by "flesh," Jesus is referring to His eventual death on the cross. And when He says we are to eat of that bread, it means that we are to trust in the breaking of His body on the cross for our salvation. We receive eternal life when we place our trust and faith in His sacrifice. (John 11:25–26 is also helpful here.)

We see clearly that eternal life begins upon belief, but you might wonder when it ends. Fortunately, even our most elementary definition of eternity applies here: it never ends. It is, as the psalmist says, "from everlasting to everlasting" (see Psalm 103:17).

Befitting something that is "from everlasting to everlasting," the Bible also tells us that eternal life cannot be taken away from us. Jesus says,

> "I give them eternal life, and they will never perish, and no one will snatch them out of my hand. My Father, who has given them to me, is greater than all, and no one is able to snatch them out of the Father's hand." *(John 10:28–29)*

What a great image! I remember when I was little, sometimes we young boys would get into arguments about whose father was biggest and strongest. (Do little boys still do that? I sure hope so!). But of course the biggest and strongest Father of all is God the Father, and Jesus assures us that since His Father is greater than all, no one is able to snatch you out of His hand. We are safe in the Father's hands, and no one (and I mean no one, not even ourselves) can wrest us away from Him. We are safe, eternally, beginning now.

Think about this too: Jesus *gives* us eternal life. It is not something that we earn. It is something we receive. And the nature of the life that Jesus gives is eternal. It cannot and will not be taken from us.

This is sometimes referred to as "eternal security" or "the perseverance of the saints." There are many verses about this (Romans 8:38 and 39 come immediately to mind; see also 1 John 5:11–13 and Romans 11:29) and it is part of the gift that God gives us when we place our trust in Jesus.

Jesus is the life, the source of it from beginning to end and in every place in-between. Let's take a look at just a few more verses to wrap up our study.

After he wrote the Gospel of John, the apostle John wrote three letters to the young church. The first of those, cleverly called 1 John in your Bible, gives us this amazing promise:

> And this is the testimony, that God gave us eternal life, and this life is in his Son. Whoever has the Son has life; whoever does not have the Son of God does not have life. *(1 John 5:11–12)*

Could he be any more clear? Without Jesus, you don't have life, eternal or otherwise. With Jesus, you do—and you have it abundantly.

The key to living, according to Paul, is Jesus. In addition to saying "for to me to live is Christ, and to die is gain" (Philippians 1:21, as mentioned earlier), he also wrote these immortal words:

> I have been crucified with Christ. It is no longer I who live, but Christ who lives in me. And the life I now live in the flesh I live by faith in the Son of God, who loved me and gave himself for me.
>
> *(Galatians 2:20)*

We need to let Jesus live through us. He and He alone needs to be the focus of our lives. And He alone is worthy of that position.

I'll conclude not just this lesson but also this series with something else that Paul wrote, this time to the church at Philippi. It sums up nicely the points we've been looking at, that Christ is God, that He came here in a fantastic way, that He cared for people like no one ever has, and that He is, indeed, the Life!

Have this mind among yourselves, which is yours in Christ Jesus, who, though he was in the form of God, did not count equality with God a thing to be grasped, but emptied himself, by taking the form of a servant, being born in the likeness of men. And being found in human form, he humbled himself by becoming obedient to the point of death, even death on a cross. Therefore God has highly exalted him and bestowed on him the name that is above every name, so that at the name of Jesus every knee should bow, in heaven and on earth and under the earth, and every tongue confess that Jesus Christ is Lord, to the glory of God the Father.   *(Philippians 2:5–11)*

Amen!

Appendix:
Verses Regarding the Deity of Christ

Jesus, the Spirit, and the Father are three in one. They are the same in their nature, not in their position. Here is a (very) partial list of verses that attest to Jesus' deity.

Matthew 1:23 (His very name is "God with us"!)
Matthew 14:33
Matthew 16:16
Matthew 28:19 (Trinitarian)
Luke 6:5
Luke 7:48 (forgiving the sinful woman)
John 1:3
John 5:18
John 8:58
John 14:8–9
Acts 2:36
Romans 10:8–9
2 Corinthians 13:14 (Trinitarian)
Philippians 2:6
Philippians 2:10
Colossians 1:15–16
Colossians 2:9–10

Titus 2:13

Hebrews 1:8

2 Peter 1:1

1 John 3:5

1 John 4:2–3

Revelation 19:16

Appendix:
The Trinity

Some people object to the idea of Jesus being God. One of the reasons they do this is because it is hard for them to grasp the idea of the Trinity.

That's understandable, as the Trinity is a unique concept. But it is thoroughly biblical. You might find the way the ESV *Study Bible* describes the Trinity to be helpful:

> The biblical teaching on the Trinity embodies four essential affirmations:
>
> 1. There is one and only one true and living God.
>
> 2. This one God eternally exists in three persons—God the Father, God the Son, and God the Holy Spirit.
>
> 3. These three persons are completely equal in attributes, each with the same divine nature.
>
> 4. While each person is *fully* and *completely* God, the persons are not identical.
>
> The differences among Father, Son, and Holy Spirit are found in the way they relate to one another and the role each plans in accomplishing their unified purpose.   (ESV *Study Bible, p. 2513*)

Believing in the Trinity does not mean that we believe in three different gods. We believe strongly, as Deuteronomy 6:4 tells us, that "The LORD our God, the LORD is one." But we believe that He exists in three "Persons"—the Father, Son, and Holy Spirit. This is not meant to be a full treatise on this subject, so you may want to do further research. A good study Bible will help you here. See also 2 Corinthians 13:14, 1 Peter 1:2, and Matthew 3:16–17 for instances of where the Three are mentioned together.

About the Author

Kit Sublett lives in Houston, Texas, where he served on the staff of Young Life for twenty years. He is the editor of numerous books as well as the author of several other books written to help people grow in their Christian faith. He considers *The Diaries of Jim Rayburn* (Young Life's founder) to be his *magnum opus*. He is a graduate of Trinity University. Follow him on Twitter @kitsublett. He can be reached through the publisher at ran@whitecapsmedia.com.

Colophon

Book designed by Randolph McMann for Whitecaps Media

Main body composed in Chaparral Pro Regular 10.5/15. Chaparral Pro was created by Adobe designer Carol Twombly

Cover designed by Stephanie W. Dicken

426 Series editor: Kit Sublett

Be sure to visit
whitecapsmedia.com
for more
426 Series Bible studies
and the Study Guide
for this book